SALAD GARDENS

A KID'S GUIDE TO GARDENING

ALEX KUSKOWSKI

Super Sandcastle

An Imprint of Abdo Publishing
www.abdopublishing.com

**Consulting Editor, Diane Craig,
M.A./Reading Specialist**

www.abdopublishing.com

Published by Abdo Publishing, a division of ABDO, PO Box 398166, Minneapolis, Minnesota 55439. Copyright © 2015 by Abdo Consulting Group, Inc. International copyrights reserved in all countries. No part of this book may be reproduced in any form without written permission from the publisher. Super SandCastle™ is a trademark and logo of Abdo Publishing.

Printed in the United States of America, North Mankato, Minnesota
102014
012015

 THIS BOOK CONTAINS RECYCLED MATERIALS

Editor: Liz Salzmann
Content Developer: Alex Kuskowski
Cover and Interior Design and Production: Mighty Media, Inc.
Photo Credits: Jen Schoeller, Shutterstock

Library of Congress Cataloging-in-Publication Data

Kuskowski, Alex.
  Super simple salad gardens : a kid's guide to gardening / Alex Kuskowski.
     pages cm. -- (Super simple gardening)
  ISBN 978-1-62403-526-5
1. Salad vegetables--Juvenile literature. 2. Vegetable gardening--Juvenile literature. I. Title. II. Series: Kuskowski, Alex. Super simple gardening.
  SB324.K872 2015
  635--dc23
                        2014023977

Super SandCastle™ books are created by a team of professional educators, reading specialists, and content developers around five essential components—phonemic awareness, phonics, vocabulary, text comprehension, and fluency—to assist young readers as they develop reading skills and strategies and increase their general knowledge. All books are written, reviewed, and leveled for guided reading, early reading intervention, and Accelerated Reader® programs for use in shared, guided, and independent reading and writing activities to support a balanced approach to literacy instruction.

TO ADULT HELPERS

• • • • • • • • •

Gardening is a lifelong skill. It is fun and simple to learn. There are a few things to remember to keep kids safe. Gardening requires commitment. Help your children stay dedicated to watering and caring for their plants. Some activities in this book recommend adult supervision. Some use sharp tools. Be sure to review the activities before starting and be ready to assist your budding gardeners when necessary.

• • • • • • • • •

Key Symbol

In this book you may see this symbol. Here is what it means.

 Outside Light
Put your plant outside.
Direct Light = in sunlight.
Indirect Light = in shade.

TABLE OF CONTENTS

GET INTO GARDENING

Dig into the world of gardening. Salad gardens are a great place to start. Growing your own food is good for the **environment**.

It is easy to start. This book will give you simple tips. Learn about the plants you can grow. Get your hands dirty. Grow something great!

SALAD GARDENS

Salad gardens are easy to create. Plant your favorite vegetables. Make fun labels for the plants. Then eat the veggies in **delicious** dishes!

GROW YOUR FOOD!

All healthy salad gardens take planning.
Edible plants need special care to
survive. Here's how to get started!

START OUTSIDE

Most salad gardens are planted outside. Learn about the vegetables you want to grow. These are some popular garden vegetables.

tomatoes   beans

lettuce   peppers

carrots   squash

Some of these plants will grow fast. Some will grow slowly. Keep a **schedule** so you'll know when your vegetables will be ripe!

tomatoes

lettuce

carrots

beans

peppers

squash

TOOLS

These are some of the important gardening tools you will be using for the projects in this book.

containers & pots

garden gloves

hand trowel

plants

soil

rocks

watering can

wood skewer & string

SAFETY

Be safe and responsible while gardening. There are a few rules for doing gardening projects.

Ask Permission

Get **permission** to do a project. You might want to use tools or things around the house. Ask first!

Be Safe

Get help from an adult when using sharp tools or moving something heavy.

Clean Up

Clean up your working area when you are finished. Put everything away.

DIG INTO DIRT

The right dirt is important for a healthy salad garden. It helps plants get the **nutrients** they need.

Choose the best soil for your plants. If you don't know, ask a gardener for help.

All-Purpose Garden Soil

This soil works best with outdoor plants. Buy soil with **peat moss** and **vermiculite**.

All-Purpose Potting Mix

This soil works well with most plants in pots. Buy soil with peat moss and vermiculite.

READY, SET, DIG!

Mix It Up

Before planting your vegetables, turn the soil. Dig in the dirt and mix it up. Take out any rocks or sticks you find.

Fertilizer

Fertilizer is food for plants! Most plants need fertilizer every few weeks. It comes in **pellets**, powder, or liquid. The package will tell you how much to use.

SEASONAL SOWING

Lettuce

Lettuce can grow all summer and into the fall.

Tomatoes

Tomato plants like the temperature just right! Wait until it is between 65 and 75 **degrees** before planting them.

Cucumbers

Cucumbers like it warm! Plant seeds or seedlings when the temperature is 65 degrees or higher.

HAPPY HARVEST!

Lettuce

Harvest the whole plant by cutting it off near the soil. Or pick the outer leaves for a small salad. The plant will keep growing!

Cherry Tomatoes

Pick tomatoes off the plant as soon as they turn red. They are ready to eat.

Cucumbers

Pick cucumbers when they are green and 6 to 8 inches (15 to 20 cm) long.

6 to 8 inches (15 to 20 cm)

Bell Peppers

Cut peppers off the vine when they are colorful. You can grow them big or small.

COOL CARE

Watering Wisdom
Plants need water. Keep the soil moist for most plants. If the soil feels dry, water your plants!

The Right Light
Light is important! Get the right light for your plants. Check how many hours of sunlight your plants need.

To get the right light check where you are going to put your plants. Does the ground get light early or late in the day? Light in the afternoon is stronger. The plants that get afternoon light will need less time in the sun.

Wonderful Weeding

Weeds can harm your plants. Check for weeds often. Pull them out. Make sure to get the roots.

Pest Detective

Check plants for bugs. Some eat plants. Other bugs help plants stay healthy. Learn about any bugs you find. Find out if they are good or bad for your plants.

SUMMER GREENS

GROW YOUR OWN SALAD!

Supplies
. . . .

rectangular planter

potting soil

hand trowel

garden gloves

ruler

1 6-pack lettuce leaf
seedlings

1 6-pack mesclun
seedlings

watering can

OUTSIDE
INDIRECT SUN

DIRECTIONS

1. Fill the planter three-fourths full with soil.

2. Dig one row of three holes. Make the holes 1 inch (5 cm) apart.

3. Take the lettuce seedlings out of their trays.

Project continues on the next page

4 Pull gently at the roots to loosen them.

5 Put a lettuce seedling in each hole. Fill the holes with soil. Press down to make the soil firm.

6 Dig another row of three holes. Make the holes 1 inch (5 cm) apart.

7. Take the mesclun seedlings out of their trays. Pull gently at the roots to loosen them.

8. Put a seedling in each hole. Fill the holes with soil. Press down to make the soil firm.

9. Add more soil to fill in any extra space in the planter. Press the soil firmly. Water the seedlings well.

COOL CARE Harvest the lettuce when it is 4 to 5 inches (10 to 13 cm) high. Wash it in water before serving.

TASTY VEGGIES

EAT HEALTHY YEAR-ROUND!

OUTSIDE
DIRECT SUN

Supplies

• • • • • • • • •

3 6-inch (15 cm) pots
stones
garden gloves
hand trowel
potting soil
1 cherry tomato
seedling
1 pepper seeding
1 cucumber seeding
wooden skewer
string
watering can
fertilizer
sharp knife
cutting board
bowl
2 tablespoons olive oil
2 tablespoons vinegar
salt & pepper

DIRECTIONS

1. Fill each pot one-quarter full with stones.

2. Fill each pot three-quarters full with soil.

3. Take the tomato seedling out of its tray. Pull gently at the roots to loosen them. Place the seedling in one pot. Add more soil to the pot.

Project continues on the next page

4 Take the pepper seedling out of its tray. Pull gently at the roots to loosen them. Place it in the second pot. Add more soil to the pot.

5 Take the cucumber seedling out of its tray. Pull gently at the roots to loosen them. Place it in the third pot. Add more soil to the pot

6 If necessary add stakes to the plants. Put a skewer in the soil near the seedling. Tie the plant to the stake with string.

COOL CARE The plants need 6 to 8 hours of sun a day. Put the plants inside if it is colder than 70 **degrees** outside.

7. Water all the plants.

8. Harvest 1 cucumber, 1 pepper, and 6 tomatoes when they are ready.

9. Wash the veggies.

10. Chop the veggies into small pieces. Put them in a bowl.

11. Add the olive oil, vinegar, salt, and pepper. Stir. Serve your tasty salad!

COOL CARE

Add **fertilizer** to the plants after 10 days. Then add fertilizer once every 2 weeks. Don't add fertilizer after veggies appear.

PLANT MARKERS

NEVER FORGET WHICH PLANT IS WHICH!

Supplies

- newspaper
- soft balsa wood
- marker
- scissors
- acrylic paint
- paintbrushes
- wooden stirring sticks
- craft glue
- sealant spray

DIRECTIONS

1. Cover your work area with newspaper.

2. Draw shapes on the balsa wood. Make each shape 2 inches (5 cm) across. Draw an **octagon**, a rectangle, and a triangle.

3. Cut out the shapes.

4. Round off the corners.

Project continues on the next page

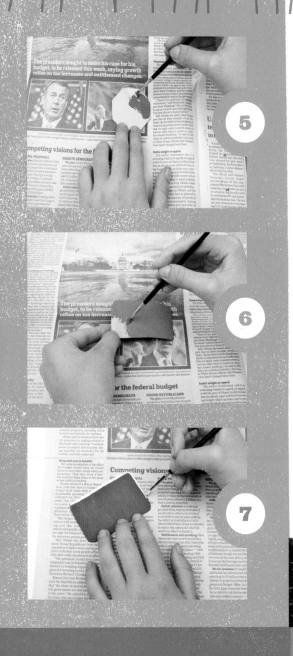

5 Paint the **octagon** red. Let the paint dry.

6 Paint the rectangle green. Paint the triangle yellow. Let the paint dry.

7 Outline the octagon and rectangle with white paint. Let the paint dry.

8 Outline the triangle with black paint. Let the paint dry.

9 Paint the names of your plants. Use the same color as the outline.

10 Glue one end of a stirring stick to the back of each sign. Let the glue dry.

11 Have an adult cover the signs with sealant spray. Let it dry. Stick the signs next to your plants.

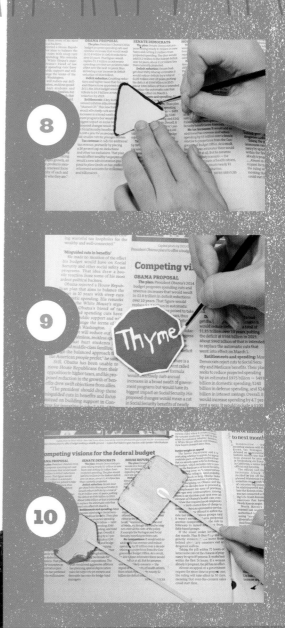

FELLOW FARMER

THIS SCARECROW WILL KEEP BIRDS AWAY!

Supplies

. . . .

newspaper

2 8-inch (20 cm) pots

1 8-inch (20 cm)
saucer

1 6-inch (15 cm) pot

blue, green, yellow
& black waterproof
paint

foam brush

paintbrush

heavy-duty glue

googly eyes

3 buttons

styrofoam disk

raffia

green chenille stems

handkerchief

small straw hat

DIRECTIONS

1   Cover your work area with newspaper.

2   Paint one of the larger pots blue.
    Paint the other larger pot green. Paint
    the **saucer** black. Let the paint dry.
    Paint a second coat if necessary.

3   Hold the smaller pot right side up.
    Glue on googly eyes. Paint a yellow
    nose. Add a black mouth. Let it dry.

4   Glue 3 buttons in a row to the green
    pot. Let the glue dry.

Project continues on the next page

5 Put glue on the bottom of the blue pot. Put glue in the **saucer**. Set the pot in the saucer. Press it down firmly.

6 Glue the rims of the 8-inch (20 cm) pots together. This is the body.

7 Glue the Styrofoam disk to the bottom of the green pot.

8 Put glue on top of the Styrofoam. Place the smaller pot right side up on top. Line the face up with buttons on the green pot. Let the glue dry 24 hours.

9 Fold 4 raffia strips until they are about 8 inches (20 cm) long.

10 Wind a chenille stem around the raffia. Start 1 inch (5 cm) from the end of the chenille stem. Stop 1 inch (5 cm) away from the end of the raffia. This is an arm.

11 Repeat steps 9 and 10 to make another arm.

12 Stick the unwound ends of the chenille stems into the Styrofoam. Put one on each side of the face.

13 Tie the handkerchief around the Styrofoam. Place the hat on the head of the scarecrow. Put it in your garden.

GLOSSARY

container – something that other things can be put into.

degree – the unit used to measure temperature.

delicious – very pleasing to taste or smell.

environment – nature and everything in it, such as the land, sea, and air.

fertilizer – something used to make plants grow better in soil.

nutrient – something that helps living things grow. Vitamins, minerals, and proteins are nutrients.

octagon – a flat shape with eight sides and eight angles.

peat moss – a type of moss that usually grows on wet land and is used in gardening.

pellet – a small, hard ball.

permission – when a person in charge says it's okay to do something.

saucer – a shallow dish that goes under something to catch spills.

schedule – a list of the times when things will happen.

vermiculite – a light material that holds water that is often added to potting soil.